Table of Contents

Dedication	iii
Introduction	1
Lost	3
Invisible	5
Chasing	7
In Between	11
Dark Heart Free Will	15
Warriors Stay	19
Gaslight	23
Headlights	27
Goodbye on a Different Day	31
Scattered	35
Lost Keys	37
Set Free	39
The Man	43
The Rise	45
About the Author	47
Contact the Author	48

THE BEAUTY IS IN THE RISE

A Collection of Breakthrough Poetic Messages

Amy L. Gaines, LCSW

The Beauty is in the Rise: A Collection of Breakthrough Poetic Messages
by Amy L. Gaines, LCSW

Cover design, editing, book layout, and publishing services by KishKnows, Inc., Richton Park, Illinois, 708-252-DOIT

admin@kishknows.com, www.kishknows.com

ISBN 978-0-578-36538-1
LCCN 2022901523

All rights reserved. No part of this book may be reproduced, distributed, or transmitted in any form or by any means, including photocopying, recording, digital scanning, or other electronic or mechanical methods, without the prior written permission of the publisher, except in the case of brief quotations embodied in critical reviews and certain other noncommercial uses permitted by copyright law. For permission requests, please contact Amy Gaines at *amylgaines@icloud.com*

Copyright © 2022 by Amy L. Gaines

Printed in the United States of America

Dedication

Dedicated to all the fierce, feisty warriors and weepers. To the strong women who have poured into me and shown me love, courage, resiliency, patience, and character throughout my life. To my mother, my grandmother, my sisters, and my friends.

To my dad, my pastor, my sons and nephews, my brothers, and my friends. The strong men, now and next, the providers and protectors. Those who had to learn the way to show the way. Your leadership and hard work; we see you quietly modeling strong character without complaining, and I dedicate this work to you. My cup runneth over when I think of those who have gone before me…are still part of me, forever and always.

To the youth, to the next. To those who will run with the vision and those that we speak to the now and future of. We see you, and we already know—you are brave, resilient, and full of hope and love. We see your zeal and enthusiasm for change. I dedicate this to you, the youth, the next. We rise in hopes to help you rise— every day. Whether you are broken or brave, you are wonderfully and fearfully made. We speak life to you. NEVER QUIT! Run, soar, and be free. BE YOU. BE BRAVE. Even when you are shaking in your brave.

Introduction

I wrote my book over a period of many years to express, heal, and be set free from a very deep pain. I often explain that "I was cut and bled these poems." I wrote my poetry to not only survive, but to *thrive*. My writing process was internal and had to be patiently waited on. I would try to force some of the writing out of a deep desperation to simply "just be healed," but just like healing is a process, the words would only come forth at each stage of breakthrough. Over time, I began to accept this, instead of wrestling with what I know as "writer's block." I have come to call some of the epiphanies "lightning bolt" revelations because throughout the process of wrestling, travailing, and feelings of being on an emotional roller coaster at times, I could be doing anything from driving in my car to work, speaking with a friend, praying, listening to music, playing outdoors with my sons, or being woken up at 2:00 a.m. when the breakthrough would come to me. It was at those points that I had lightning bolt revelations…which is my way of saying that the work had been done, and the manifestation hit suddenly when I was least expecting it. The poems are part of my personal use of an evidence-based form of therapy called "narrative therapy;" and although I began writing in sixth grade which was many years before I knew anything about therapy, it was already a work in progress. With each poem, I have given a simple explanation of the story it tells; but overall, in order to do the inner work, it is open to the personal interpretation of the reader. In all honesty, during the times that I did not know how to live, I held tight to my writing and the Scripture and knowing about beauty from ashes. I had an inner knowing that there was a greater purpose for everything. I wrote my book because I refused to quit; to become better and not bitter, to heal and be set free so that I could continue to help and empower others. I wrote to live, to find my voice, and to love myself despite myself. I wrote my book to be an example of strength yet to be transparent and true, never perfect but always a work in progress. I wrote my book to never get stuck in self-pity or victimhood but to stand in my victory and RISE, and to encourage, inspire, and guide others along the way. It is my prayer that my readers will come to know the power of God through a personal relationship, prayer, and study of His Word because no other words that I or any other human being could ever write would be truer and more life giving. It is the study of HIS Word and knowing Him that has allowed the transformation of my life. If He did it for me, He most certainly can and will do it for you.

Lost

Packed inside a box of lies

Can you see it in my eyes

Looking for the missing piece

To a puzzle that is incomplete.

Finding the pieces to make me whole

As I search for my soul.

I brought you into this maze

Then it blew up in my face

You always were a good disguise

For the pieces missing inside

It was easier to hide than to heal

Even if the puzzle was not real

It was there for the world to see

And no one even knew…

It was not me.

Reflection and Breakthrough

***Lost** was written about identity crisis and self-discovery during adolescence. Have you ever had an identity crisis or gone through a period of self-discovery? Reflect on that time here.*

_____

_____

_____

_____

_____

_____

_____

_____

_____

_____

_____

_____

_____

_____

_____

_____

Invisible

Maybe it comes from years of
not being heard.

Whether by others or by ignoring
the whisper inside.

That sort of awareness of your
every word.

Desperately grasping for the
knowledge that someone hears.

Desperately seeking approval in
someone's eyes.

Every syllable another attempt at
redemption.

The day should come that you
only seek such approval

Staring back from the mirror.

That comes from either being
wiser and self-actualized

Or older and exhilarated.

At the end of the day, that
approval you were desperately seeking

Is the beginning of merely a flash
of a face that is no longer there.

Reflection and Breakthrough

***Invisible** was written about seeking external validation and the process of finding one's voice. From where do you seek your validation? Have you found your voice? What does it sound like?*

_____
_____
_____
_____
_____
_____
_____
_____
_____
_____
_____
_____
_____
_____
_____
_____

Chasing

Happy endings right off a cliff

Ripping, roaring

Sliding, gliding

Don't lose your grip!

Parachute free fall

Let it rip!

Full throttle over the edge

Blazing…chasing…craving…

Shaky ledge

Manic locomotive

Full steam ahead!

Crushing…crying…

Paragliding…into the red.

Zone of frantic panic

Pump the brakes

Cover the scrapes

Bandage the bleeding.

Soldier up

Too great to be tragic

But spare me the madness…

I want *off* the pain train.

Next stop

Finally free

Yet I can hear the whistle blow

All aboard the next shit show!

Reflection and Breakthrough

Chasing *was written about seeking love in unhealthy ways and reoccurring patterns. Have you identified unhealthy and reoccurring patterns in your life? How do you "flip the script"?*

_____

_____

_____

_____

_____

_____

_____

_____

_____

_____

_____

_____

_____

_____

_____

_____

In Between

Your love was better in a dream

Start to finish and in between

Place unfinished

Story untold

Eternal hold

Stay

Just one more day

Eternal bliss

A cannot miss

With a twist

Love a blank slate

Fits into a soulmate

Shipwreck…what the heck

Let it crash and collide

Eyes open wide

It's a free fall

A strange ride

Empty well

Butterflies and tears

But what the hell!

Fight, *flight*, **freeze**

Take you to your knees

One says you're undone

You're not the one

But the blank slate

Written on until you seal your fate

Love in the mirror.

Reflection and Breakthrough

***In Between** was written about pain, escapism, and letting go. What are you seeking to escape from?*

Dark Heart Free Will

Dark heart

Fake light grew dim

Never real

Dark art inside yourself

You cannot feel

The truth of your hate

Revealed

Dark heart

Stuck in fear

Lies inside yourself

Ended there

Empty last one

You are the end

Incomplete but finished

As your light grew dim

Your truth

You will know well

In the empty

Always and after

Of your free will

A light will appear…

But only to reveal

How the dark really feels.

Moments of this world's escape

You hold tight

Your free will

Dark as night.

Light heart, free will

Time in the dark

To be still.

Dark clouds passed through

The winds grew and grew

Grey faded into blue.

Forcing the light to bend

But never break

Left was all that is real

nothing of that which is fake.

Pieces of your first heart

Your unfinished art

Needed to fill

Always and after

Free will.

Reflection and Breakthrough

Dark Heart Free Will *was written about feeling abandoned, afraid, and angry. Have you ever felt abandoned? What are the emotions that came with that feeling?*

_____

_____

_____

_____

_____

_____

_____

_____

_____

_____

_____

_____

_____

_____

_____

Warriors Stay

Spirits rise

They do not run.

The easy path never ends

But the one less chosen

Always wins.

And your wheels continue to turn

The same old way.

Another day after day

Until they come undone.

Only now, there is only one

The spirit does not run.

Fight or flight

Face the facts

And end your meaningless attacks.

The weapons of this world you choose

Defeat is near when the weapon is *you*.

Run if you must.

You're lost without trust.

All your weapons have turned to dust.

Until you fall with clouds in your eyes

You are left to your own demise.

Then you will see

That the fight was already lost.

Because in the end

You ran at any cost.

On your knees

You will meet

The spirit inside of me.

With rain in your eyes

Now you finally see

The *Beauty* is in the *Rise*.

Reflection and Breakthrough

Warriors Stay *was written about running, betrayal, and hypocrisy. How do those three concepts relate to one another? How do they fit into your story?*

_____
_____
_____
_____
_____
_____
_____
_____
_____
_____
_____
_____
_____
_____
_____
_____
_____

Gaslight

These fools.

These friends.

These foes.

These Janes…

John Does

Lie to your face

Set the pace.

You betray

Your only friend

You die inside

Cry out "WHY"

End up at the place

Where you

Started.

Stopped.

Stood still.

Losing your will

Be true.

Oh, so fake

Lost in your fate.

You say, "I am this, I am that."

BUT

"I am *fearless*."

"I am *woke*."

While you shake in your almost.

Teeter on the edge of brave

Only to rage fast to get away.

All I say is "Choose the way."

Left.

Right.

Scream.

Fight.

Flee.

Freeze.

You.

Me.

Go.

Stay.

Just get the hell away

All I say

Is *SAY.*

"I. am. brave."

Reflection and Breakthrough

***Gaslight** is about seeing through the tactic of projecting a false image by tearing others down, hypocrisy, and manipulation. Have you ever been gaslighted? Reflect on the emotions that this experience produced.*

_____

_____

_____

_____

_____

_____

_____

_____

_____

_____

_____

_____

_____

_____

_____

_____

Headlights

Waiting for headlights

With every light around the

curve

A nudge of hope

With every glimmer

The light got bigger

Closer it seemed

Until it rushed by my dream

Wait! Another!

This is it! The one!

Until…it wasn't

Passed right by

With a tear in my eye

That never dropped

And the light never stopped

Right where

Right there!

It came and went…

But the pain was never in vain

And the tears never stained

Even when they fell like rain

The light never died

No matter how hard I cried

Even when I ran and screamed

The light kept my dreams

Tucked away

So still and safe

For the day

A day like today

When I would say

The light was inside

And just like that…

I stopped

Watching for headlights.

Reflection and Breakthrough

Headlights *deals with disappointments, reoccurring patterns, and seeking external validation. What patterns (good or bad) do you see in your life right now?*

_____

_____

_____

_____

_____

_____

_____

_____

_____

_____

_____

_____

_____

_____

_____

Goodbye on a Different Day

Had I known

You were almost gone

I would have walked away

A little slower that day

How did I miss

The goodbye in your kiss

The last wave on your face

That said you finished your race

The last pull of that door

The last step on the floor

The last ride in the wind

The goodbye

My friend.

Had I known

Goodbye and gone

Now here I write

As you're out of sight

But a breeze of cold air

A brush of my hair

Only…you're not there

Had I known

I would have captured it

To be still

And daydream it's not real

Frozen in time

Crying *"Rewind!"*

Reach into the past

Make it last

Never to be found screaming

"Turn around!"

I'm just dreaming

Stop right there

Just let me stare

Freeze while I dream

I go away to that place

Where there is no time

No space

And *goodbye* is on a different day.

Reflection and Breakthrough

Goodbye on a Different Day *was written about grief and loss and not wanting to let go. How do you process grief in your own life?*

Scattered

Only thing that mattered

Broken blazing breeze

Off to sea

Take flight

This night

Go rushing wind and leap

Just get the hell out of my sleep

You are not real

You don't feel

You came to conquer the fear,

Blissfully brave

Hidden in a cave

Obsessed with a goodbye wave

That never came

Little girl, fly on.

Don't expect me to be your home.

You will be strong after a while.

Reflection and Breakthrough

***Scattered** was written about pain that keeps a person up at night. What keeps you awake at night? How do you put it to rest so that you can rest?*

_____

_____

_____

_____

_____

_____

_____

_____

_____

_____

_____

_____

_____

_____

_____

_____

_____

_____

Lost Keys

Blame it on the ADD

But Jesus set me free.

From the other side

He said

Don't hide

Your pain is never in vain

The Kingdom is never lost—

I reign!

But I lost my keys again

my friend.

I love how imperfectly

perfect

you are.

A bright shiny star.

I created the keys

Exactly the way that would

glorify me.

No two are the same.

Reflection and Breakthrough

***Lost Keys** was written after I went through a period of self-defeating thoughts and condemning myself for being different. What are the lies that you have told yourself about being different?*

_____

_____

_____

_____

_____

_____

_____

_____

_____

_____

_____

_____

_____

_____

_____

_____

Set Free

Take a breath

There's nothing left

Break me to set yourself free

Throw yourself on the fire

Oh, but the devil is a liar

I return it to the sender

And stand on the rock of my defender.

Your words fly over my head

I am alive and not dead

Who I am has *nothing* to do with all you said.

I already ate my daily bread

Like a word wrapped around me

He already found me.

You look but you cannot see

Your hate will not break me

I lay it down at Jesus' feet.

Your force pushes me to my secret place

Where I look into my Father's face.

He tells me His heart

To reverse the fiery dart

He sets me free

Planted like a tree

He says, Draw near to me.

Your heart is in my hand

I love you, my friend.

Go ahead and fly

Soar above the sky.

Touch my wind of freedom

Let's run to the Kingdom

With faith to see

All you are in me.

Reflection and Breakthrough

***Set Free** deals with rejection, surrender, and deliverance. Discuss these themes (perhaps they are one theme?) in your own life.*

The Man

My worth is not in a man

When this is all part of

THE man's plan.

I am beautiful

I am full of light

Only because of who I am in Christ.

I can't see a way

Oh, but HE can

And HE says through HIM

OH YES, WE CAN!

You see…of this world

I am not.

HIS promises

I have not forgot.

I Am HIS

And HE is mine.

Forever.

For all time.

Reflection and Breakthrough

__The Man__ was written as the last of several poems that dealt with seeking love. What themes do you see here that resonate in your own heart?

The Rise

The curvature of the weakened stem

The pull to the dirt and dew

Hanging of the lost face

The dark and damp view

Color fading away from the sun

A wilted and worn hue

My source…my light…my love…

Transforms to a different view

A rising and radiant hue

To be still and silent is what I must do

Reflections of light in the dirt and the dew

Sent to remind that the source will renew

The winds carry the light back to its place

Raising the face

A brighter and warmer hue

Having experienced a different view

Reflection and Breakthrough

The Rise *was written after seeing the beauty in a field of out-of-season sunflowers. Think of a time when you saw beauty where someone else could not, and reflect on that here.*

_____

_____

_____

_____

_____

_____

_____

_____

_____

_____

_____

_____

_____

_____

_____

About the Author

Amy L. Gaines, LCSW, is a native of Pulaski, Tennessee and grew up in Madison, Mississippi. She is a licensed clinical social worker and holds both a bachelor's and a master's degree in social work.

Amy provides individualized psychotherapy services to children and families at her private practice. She also provides supervision, consultation, advocacy, and mentorship services. Her overall purpose is to help people discover and remember who they truly are. She does this by assisting in the transformation of communities through individuals and families who are working hard to break generational cycles of oppression, trauma, and poverty. She is a humanitarian who strives to see love, diversity, and unity among people.

Amy loves to read and considers herself a lifelong learner. She also loves music and nature. She currently resides in Flora, Mississippi and is a single mother to two uniquely gifted boys, Owen and Daniel, who inspire her beyond words.

Contact the Author

If you would like to contact the author,
you may do so at:

http://thebeautyisintherise.com

thebeautyisintherise@icloud.com